SAXOPHONE POCKETBOOK

by Bill Bay

©1981 BY MEL BAY PUBLICATIONS INC., PACIFIC, MO.
INTERNATIONAL COPYRIGHT SECURED. ALL RIGHTS RESERVED.
PRINTED IN U.S.A.

PARTS OF THE SAXOPHONE

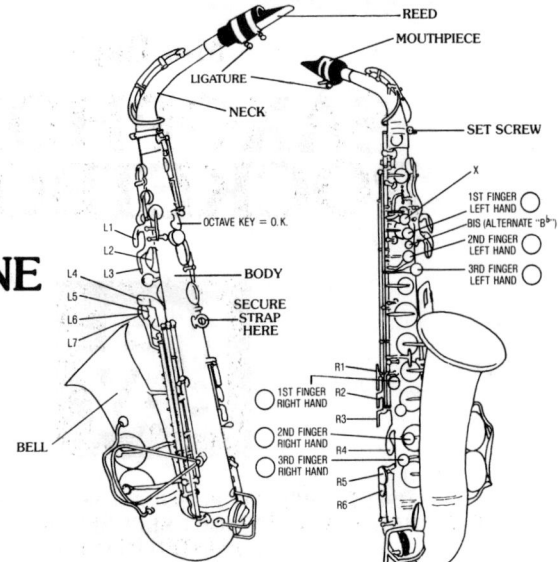

HOW TO READ FINGERING CHART

TO PLAY "G" NOTE, FOR EXAMPLE

- ● INDICATES KEY PRESSED DOWN.
- ○ INDICATES KEY NOT PRESSED DOWN.

O.K. ●
● THE FIRST THREE KEYS ARE PRESSED
● DOWN BY THE FIRST THREE FINGERS OF
— THE LEFT HAND.
○
○ THE BOTTOM THREE KEYS FOR THE RIGHT
○ HAND ARE NOT DEPRESSED.
○

O.K. INDICATES OCTAVE KEY PRESSED DOWN. (Use Thumb Left Hand)

BIS INDICATES ALTERNATE "B♭" FINGERING. (Use First Finger — Left Hand)

LETTERS AND NUMBERS INDICATE KEYS TO BE DEPRESSED.

EXAMPLE
(R1=RIGHT HAND, FIRST KEY)
(L1=LEFT HAND, FIRST KEY)

X INDICATES FIRST AND SECOND KEYS ARE DEPRESSED USING THE FIRST FINGER OF THE LEFT HAND.

SAXOPHONE FINGERING CHART

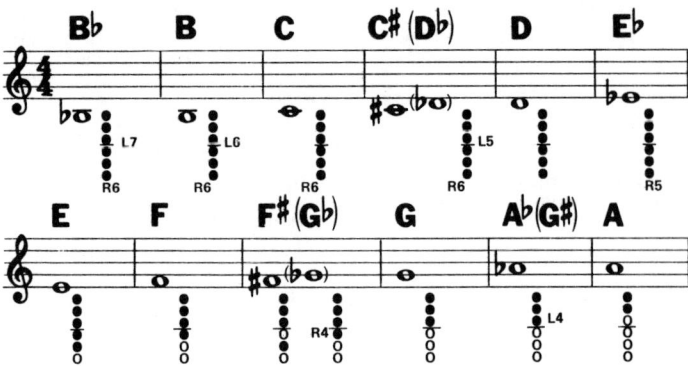

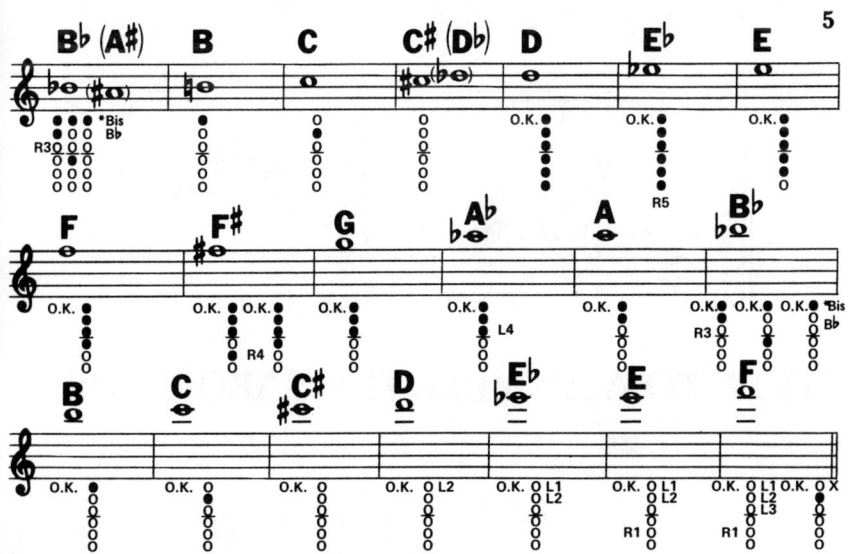

*Bis "B♭" = Press both keys with 1st. Finger.

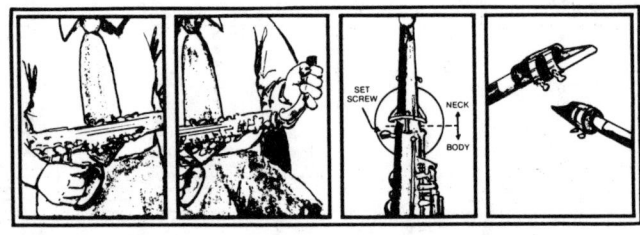

Fig. 1 *Fig. 2* *Fig. 3* *Fig. 4*

HOW TO ASSEMBLE THE SAXOPHONE

We begin by making sure that both ends of the neck are well greased. This will enable the body, neck and mouthpiece to fit together easily. The bell portion of the body should rest comfortably on the lap as shown in Figure 1. Now, holding the neck near the cork with the left hand, slip it into the saxophone body as shown in Figure 2. Remember to apply a minimum of pressure. Never force the parts of the instrument together. To make certain that the neck is positioned properly, align the back of the Octave key as shown in Figure 3. Make sure to tighten the set screw to secure the neck in place. Now, using the left hand place the mouthpiece on the neck as shown in Figure 4.

CARE OF THE SAXOPHONE

The saxophone should be oiled periodically. This is done most easily by using a toothpick and by putting key oil on the various working mechanisms. Key oil may be purchased at your local music store. Be sure to use it sparingly. Make certain that you do not bump the keys and playing mechanism of the saxophone against chairs, tables, etc. When not playing the saxophone, it is always best to place it back in its case. Make certain that you place the instrument in its case properly and never force the case shut, for this will bend keys.

It is a good idea to have a skilled repairman check your instrument for proper alignment and seating of the keys about once a year. Occasionally, pads will need to be replaced. A skilled repairman will be able to do this for you. Most music centers have repair departments.

Saxophone swabs are available and it is a very good idea to buy one and to run a saxophone swab through your instrument before putting it back in its case. This will remove excess moisture from the inside of the saxophone.

You may also want to purchase a mouthpiece brush and clean out the inside of your mouthpiece periodically.

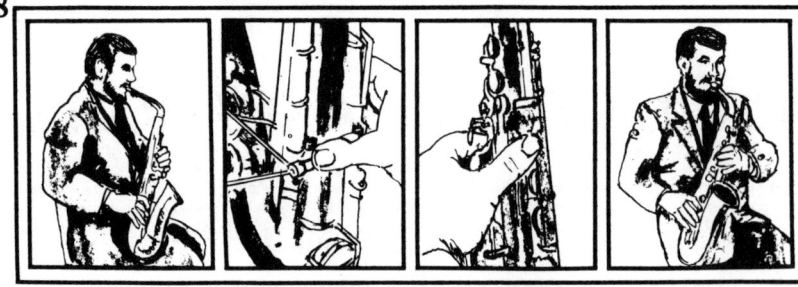

Fig. 5 Fig. 6 Fig. 7 Fig. 8

HOW TO HOLD THE SAXOPHONE

To secure the Saxophone, hook the neck strap to the instrument and place the strap around your neck, Figure 5. Next, put the thumb of the right hand underneath the lower hook as shown in Figure 6. Now, place your left hand thumb on the button below the octave key, see Figure 7. Bring the saxophone mouthpiece to your mouth by adjusting the neck strap, as shown in Figure 8.

PROPER PLAYING POSITION

Notice the positioning of the elbows in Figures 5 & 8. They should not be held against the body in a rigid manner. Rather, they are extended slightly away from the body in a relaxed way. Your back should be straight when playing and the lower part of your back should touch the chair. Do not, however, sit in a rigid position. Your body, when playing, should remain in an upright position for good breathing but you should never feel stiff. Tense body position will restrict your breathing.

TYPES OF NOTES

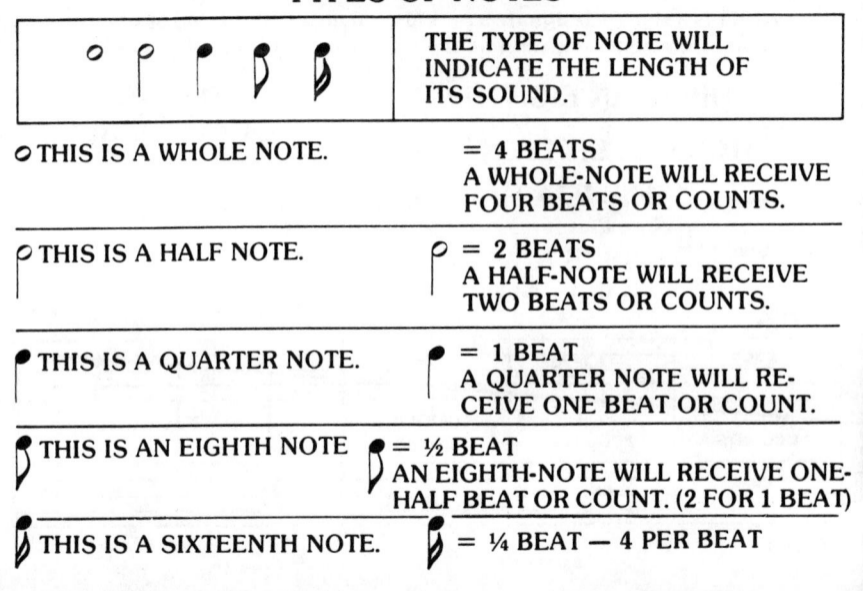

♩ ♩ ♩ ♪ ♪	THE TYPE OF NOTE WILL INDICATE THE LENGTH OF ITS SOUND.

○ THIS IS A WHOLE NOTE.   ○ = 4 BEATS
A WHOLE-NOTE WILL RECEIVE FOUR BEATS OR COUNTS.

♩ THIS IS A HALF NOTE.   ♩ = 2 BEATS
A HALF-NOTE WILL RECEIVE TWO BEATS OR COUNTS.

♩ THIS IS A QUARTER NOTE.   ♩ = 1 BEAT
A QUARTER NOTE WILL RECEIVE ONE BEAT OR COUNT.

♪ THIS IS AN EIGHTH NOTE   ♪ = ½ BEAT
AN EIGHTH-NOTE WILL RECEIVE ONE-HALF BEAT OR COUNT. (2 FOR 1 BEAT)

♪ THIS IS A SIXTEENTH NOTE.   ♪ = ¼ BEAT — 4 PER BEAT

RESTS

A REST is a sign to designate a period of silence. This period of silence will be of the same duration as the note to which it corresponds.

𝟳 **THIS IS AN EIGHTH REST**

𝟳 **THIS IS A SIXTEENTH REST**

𝄽 **THIS IS A QUARTER REST**

▬ **THIS IS A HALF REST**
Note that it lays on the line.

▬ **THIS IS A WHOLE REST**
Note that it hangs down from the line.

NOTES

WHOLE	HALF	QUARTER	EIGHTH	SIXTEENTH
4 COUNTS	2 COUNTS	1 COUNT	2 FOR 1 COUNT	4 FOR 1 COUNT

RESTS

THE TIME SIGNATURE

  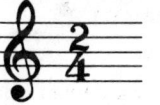 

The above examples are the common types of time signatures to be used in this book.

4 The top number indicates the number of beats per measure
4 The bottom number indicates the type of note receiving one beat beats per measure

4 beats per measure
4 a quarter-note receives one beat.

6 BEATS PER MEASURE
8 EACH EIGHTH-NOTE RECEIVES ONE FULL BEAT
(See p. 26 & 27)

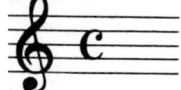 Signifies so called "common time" and is simply another way of designating $\frac{4}{4}$ time.

12   DOTTED QUARTER NOTES
A DOT AFTER A NOTE increases its Value by ONE-HALF.

DOTTED 1/4-NOTE  **EQUAL TO** 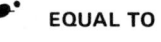 **THREE EIGHTHS** The count for the dotted quarter-note is as follows

THE TIE   The tie is a curved line that connects one or more notes. When a tie occurs, you hold the note for the combined value of the two notes tied together. You will tongue only the first note. The second note is merely held and not tongued.

SLUR   DOTTED HALF NOTE

A slur looks like this:

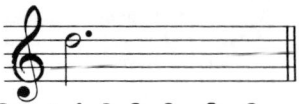

To slur, tongue the 1st note and then finger only (Don't Tongue) the succeeding notes.   Count: 1 & 2 & 3 &

TEMPO MARKINGS

Ritard . . . . Slow down gradually   *Moderato* . . . . Medium Tempo
Accellerando . . . . . Speed up gradually   *Largo* . . . . Very slow
Andante . . . . Play slowly   *Vivace* . . . . Very fast
Allegro . . . . Moderately fast   *A Tempo* . . . . Back to original tempo
                                                                                    (after slowing down or speeding up)

DYNAMIC MARKINGS

	pp	**p**	**mp**	**mf**	**f**	**ff**
Italian	Pianissimo	Piano	Mezzo piano	Mezzo Forte	Forte	Fortissimo
English	Very soft	Soft	Medium Soft	Medium loud. Normal playing volume.	Bold, strong tone.	Very loud, but controlled. Never blaring.

p ———————< | *f* ———————>

Crescendo | *Decrescendo*
Start soft and gradually increase the air until a volume of F (Forte) is reached. | Gradually decrease air flow until volume of P (Piano) is reached.

Crescendos and decrescendos are accomplished by gradually increasing or decreasing the air flow. Make certain that the tone does not waver in the process, only the level of air flow changes. The position of the tongue and lips should remain constant and there should be no variance in the pitch or quality of the tone.

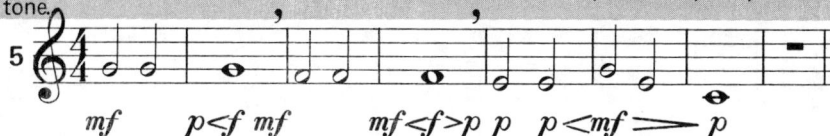

TONE AND SLUR STUDIES

EMBOUCHURE AND FINGERING STUDIES

TONGUING STUDIES

ARPEGGIOS

2 octave study

DOTTED 8ths AND 16ths

A Dotted eighth note followed by a 16th note is a common figure in music. Practice the following study until the timing is felt and understood.

STUDY

All are played the same

BATTLE HYMN OF THE REPUBLIC

HAUL AWAY JOE

Sea Song

GOBLINS

THE TRIPLET

A Triplet is a group of 3 notes, played in the time of 2 notes of the same kind.

MARCH MILITAIRE

SAX ETUDE

SAX BLUES

JAZZ SAX STUDY

24 CHROMATIC SCALE STUDIES

Repeat 8 times

O FOR A THOUSAND TONGUES TO SING

DUET
Boldly

Arr. by Bill Bay

MAJOR SCALES

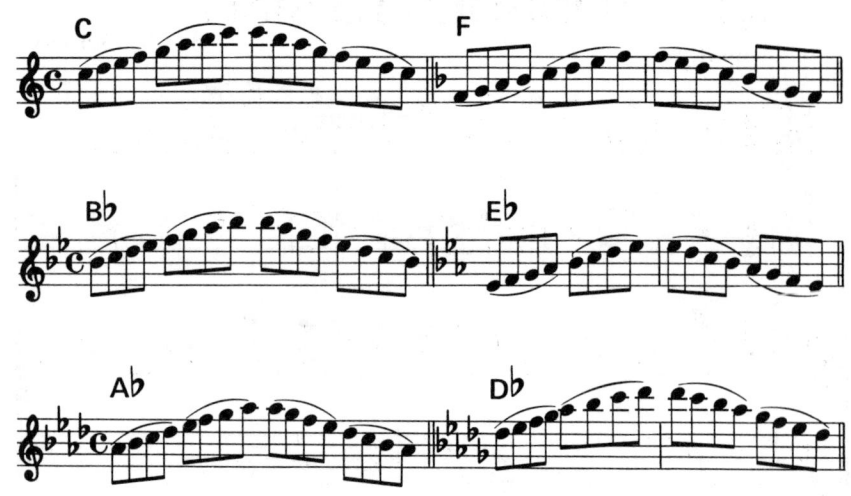

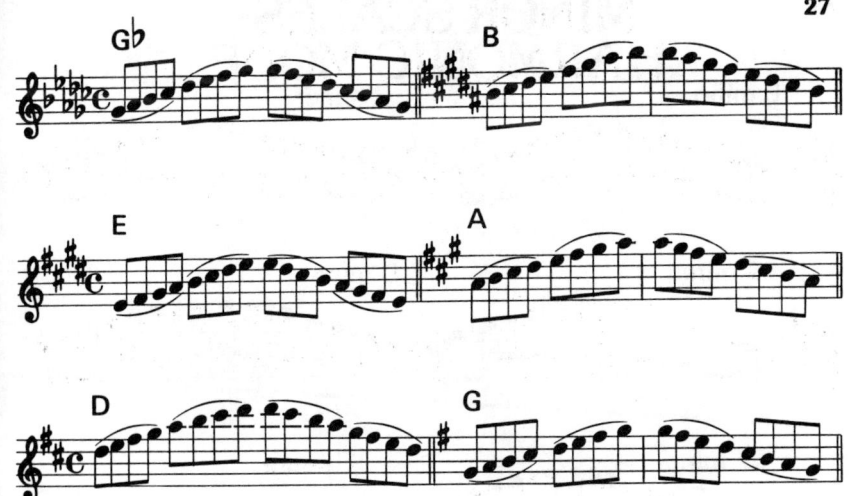

MINOR SCALES- HARMONIC MODE

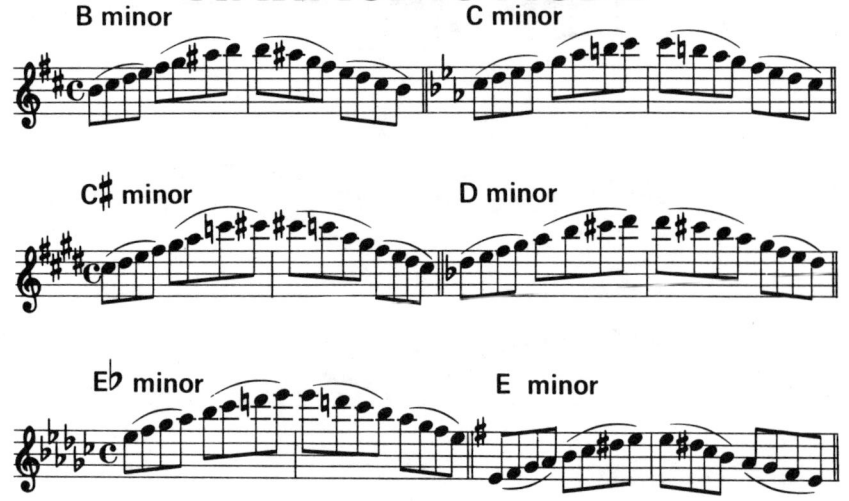

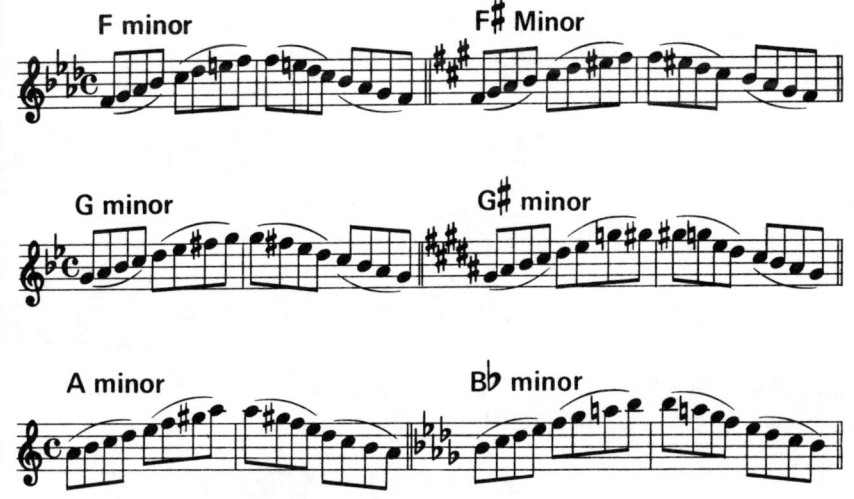

SYNCOPATION

Syncopation means to accent beats that are not normally accented. Syncopation is the basis for much popular music, rock, jazz, ragtime, etc.

TALLIS CANNON